REALITY TV TITANS

PIONEER PRACTICES WITH
Ree Drummond

Jill C. Wheeler

Checkerboard
Library

An Imprint of Abdo Publishing
abdopublishing.com

abdopublishing.com

Published by Abdo Publishing, a division of ABDO, PO Box 398166, Minneapolis, Minnesota 55439.
Copyright © 2016 by Abdo Consulting Group, Inc. International copyrights reserved in all countries.
No part of this book may be reproduced in any form without written permission from the publisher.
Checkerboard Library™ is a trademark and logo of Abdo Publishing.

Printed in the United States of America, North Mankato, Minnesota

062015
092015

THIS BOOK CONTAINS
RECYCLED MATERIALS

Design: Jen Schoeller, Mighty Media, Inc.
Production: Mighty Media, Inc.
Series Editor: Liz Salzmann
Cover Photos: Jim Wieland/Reader's Digest Association, front cover; Alamy, back cover
Interior Photos: Alamy, pp. 19, 27; Corbis, p. 29; Getty Images, pp. 5, 21; Jim Wieland/Reader's Digest
Association, pp. 11, 15, 23, 25; Mighty Media, Inc., p. 17; Seth Poppel/Yearbook Library, pp. 6, 7;
Shutterstock, pp. 3, 9, 13

Library of Congress Cataloging-in-Publication Data

Wheeler, Jill C., 1964-
  Pioneer practices with Ree Drummond / Jill C. Wheeler.
    pages cm. -- (Reality TV titans)
  Includes index.
  ISBN 978-1-62403-819-8
1. Drummond, Ree--Juvenile literature. 2. Oklahoma--Biography--Juvenile literature. 3. Ranch life--
Oklahoma--Osage County--Juvenile literature. I. Title.
F701.D78W47 2016
976.6'2504092--dc23
  [B]
                    2015009692

CONTENTS

Ree Drummond

Ree Drummond is the author, **blogger**, photographer, and writer known as the Pioneer Woman. She turned an unexpected twist in her life into a successful business. Drummond never planned to marry a rancher and live in the country. Yet she went from a city-dwelling single woman to a ranch wife and mother. This transformation is exactly what caught the attention of her many fans.

Drummond's fame began with a blog. It includes stories and photos of Drummond's life on the ranch. The blog won 16 Weblog Awards ("Bloggies") between 2007 and 2013. Today, it registers millions of page views per month.

Drummond's blog led to best-selling cookbooks, a **memoir**, several children's books, and a program on the Food Network. All reflect Drummond's sense of humor and naturally engaging style. Week after week, she turns the stuff of ordinary life into a magical world. It is a place where her readers love to escape for a while.

Drummond started her blog about ten years after getting married and moving to a ranch.

Doctor's Daughter

Ree Drummond was born Ann-Marie Smith on January 6, 1969, in Bartlesville, Oklahoma. She was the third of William and Gerre Smith's four children. She has two older brothers, Doug and Mike, and a younger sister, Betsy. Ree came by her nickname when her brother Mike could not pronounce "Marie." Mike called her "Wee-Wee." Drummond's parents changed it to "Ree-Ree." The name stuck.

Ree's father was an **orthopedic surgeon**. Her mother was a stay-at-home mom. The Drummonds lived in a wealthy area. Their home was on a golf course. Ree's early days were filled with school, ballet classes, and activities at

Ree's senior yearbook portrait

Ree *(left)* enjoyed Oklahoma as a child, but she had big-city dreams.

the local country club. In the summer, the family vacationed at South Carolina's famous Hilton Head area.

   Although she had a privileged **lifestyle**, Ree could barely wait to leave Oklahoma. She graduated from Bartlesville High School in 1987. Then she headed to Los Angeles, California, the biggest city she could think of.

California Girl

Within a week of arriving, Drummond visited all the theme parks in Los Angeles. She could not wait to explore what the city had to offer. Oklahoma quickly became a distant memory.

Drummond's time in California was not all theme parks and adventures. She also attended the University of Southern California (USC). She started out majoring in broadcast **journalism**. Later, Drummond switched her major to **gerontology**.

Drummond graduated from college in 1991. Her first job was with a company that sold products for senior citizens. Drummond worked with celebrity guests at trade shows where the products were sold.

Throughout college and her first career, Drummond loved the Los Angeles **lifestyle**. She became a **vegetarian**. She loved going to restaurants, eating **sushi**, and buying designer shoes. Although Drummond was happy in California, she started planning the next phase of her life. She decided to go to law school. But first she wanted to spend some time with her family in Oklahoma.

Drummond enjoyed hiking to the famous Hollywood sign in the Hollywood Hills.

Coming Home

Drummond left Los Angeles and returned to Bartlesville. She spent time with her family. She also started studying for the Law School Admission Test (LSAT). All students applying to law school must take the LSAT. Drummond thought she would go to law school in Chicago, Illinois. She wanted to try living in another big city.

But one night, Drummond went out with some friends from high school. She met an interesting man and struck up a conversation with him. His name was Ladd Drummond, and he was a cowboy. The two eventually started dating. They fell in love and were married on September 21, 1996.

The Drummonds went on a **honeymoon** to Australia. Ladd wanted to see how the cowboys there lived and worked. Upon returning home, the couple settled down on Ladd's cattle ranch near Pawhuska, Oklahoma. The ranch has been in the Drummond family for four generations. It is one of the largest ranches in the state. It has about 4,000 cattle and 2,000 wild horses.

The Drummond
ranch covers
nearly 40 square
miles
(101 sq km).

Ranch Life

After getting married and moving to the ranch, the next few years saw many changes in Drummond's life. Her and Ladd's daughter Alex was born in June 1997. Another daughter, Paige, followed in October 1999. Their son Bryce was born in September 2002. In June 2004, the Drummonds welcomed their second son, Todd.

Life on the ranch was very different from Drummond's former life in Los Angeles. Drummond stopped being a **vegetarian**. She started enjoying the beef from cattle raised on the ranch. Days on the ranch started early, and the work was hard. Evenings were for resting, not for going out to restaurants and staying up late.

And actually, there weren't many places to go! The ranch was far from restaurants and shops. Going anywhere required a long drive. This **isolation** was one reason why the Drummonds decided to homeschool their children. When Alex started kindergarten, her school was nearly 20 miles (32 km) away. She spent almost three hours a day on a school bus going to and from school. Drummond

After she began eating beef again, Drummond liked to make beef stew on cold winter days.

researched how homeschooling worked. It seemed like a good fit for their family. So she and Ladd decided to teach their kids at home.

A Blog Is Born

Drummond had already been busy caring for her home and family on the ranch. Once she began homeschooling the children, her days became even busier. But on May 4, 2006, Drummond found herself with several hours alone in the house. Normally she would use free time to do housework or research homeschooling ideas. But this time was different. Drummond decided to start a **blog** that day.

Drummond titled her blog *Confessions of a Pioneer Woman*. She began writing about her move from California to Oklahoma. She posted poems she had written and pictures of her children. She wrote about news from the ranch.

Drummond never expected anyone to read her blog, except maybe her mother. To Drummond's surprise, it was a hit. More and more people started reading it. Blogging became another part of Drummond's busy life on the ranch.

DID YOU KNOW?
Drummond uses part of her advertising budget to buy giveaway prizes for her readers.

Drummond
with her children,
(*clockwise from left*)
Alex, Todd, Paige,
and Bryce

The Pioneer Woman

Time passed, and *Confessions of a Pioneer Woman* kept gaining readers. Though the **blog** featured her family, Drummond did not use their real names. Readers did not care. They loved reading about the ranch and the Drummond family. They also loved the recipes and beautiful photos Drummond shared.

Confessions of a Pioneer Woman received the Best Kept Secret Award at the 2007 Weblog Awards. Two years later, the blog took top honors as Weblog of the Year. It would earn the award for the next two years.

In 2009, Drummond realized the food section of her blog was very popular. So, she launched a free community website she called Tasty Kitchen. There, she invited people to submit their favorite recipes. Tasty Kitchen has become a favorite website for people who want to share recipes. People can also promote their own food blogs and communicate with one another.

Inspired by Ree Drummond

Cheesy Cornbread

Serves 4 to 8

Ingredients

- ¼ **cup butter, softened**
- **3 tablespoons sugar**
- **2 eggs**
- **½ cup sour cream**
- **½ cup milk**
- **1 cup all-purpose flour**
- **1 cup yellow cornmeal**
- **1½ teaspoons baking powder**
- **½ teaspoon salt**
- **¼ teaspoon baking soda**
- **½ cup shredded cheddar cheese**

1. Ask an adult for help.

2. Preheat the oven to 425 degrees.

3. Put the butter and sugar in a large bowl. Stir until smooth.

4. Stir the eggs into the batter one at a time. Stir in the milk and sour cream.

5. Add the dry ingredients. Stir just until combined. Don't stir too much. The batter should be slightly lumpy.

6. **Fold** in the shredded cheddar cheese.

7. Pour the batter into a greased baking dish.

8. Bake for 20 to 25 minutes, until golden brown and crispy at the edges.

Creating Cookbooks

In 2008, Drummond started her own website. It's called The Pioneer Woman. It includes her *Confessions of a Pioneer Woman* **blog**. It also has separate sections titled "Cooking," "Home & Garden," "Homeschooling," and "Entertainment."

In October 2009, Drummond published her first cookbook. It's called *The Pioneer Woman Cooks: Recipes from an Accidental Country Girl*. The book includes recipes featured on her website. They are the kinds of recipes busy people want to serve their families. Photos and detailed instructions make the book especially helpful for beginning cooks. The book also includes Drummond's own humorous stories. It reached number one on the *New York Times* Best Sellers list.

Drummond has since published two more cookbooks. *The Pioneer Woman Cooks: Food from My Frontier* came out in 2012. It features more family-meal recipes. *The Pioneer Woman Cooks: A Year of Holidays* came out in 2013. It focuses on food for holidays and celebrations.

Drummond experiments with recipes for her cookbooks.

More Books

Drummond's cookbooks and **blog** aren't her only writing projects. Between cookbooks, she also published a **memoir**. It's called *The Pioneer Woman: Black Heels to Tractor Wheels—a Love Story*. The book is about her romance and early life with her husband. It includes many of the blog posts she wrote about their relationship. The memoir was published in 2011 and became a best seller.

Ladd isn't the only member of the family that inspired Drummond to write a book. The family's **basset hound**, Charlie, did too! In 2011, Drummond worked with illustrator Diane DeGroat to create a book about Charlie. It is called *Charlie the Ranch Dog*. In the story, Charlie thinks he is watching over the ranch and all its animals. In reality, he mostly just naps. Drummond and DeGroat turned the book into a series. The tenth Charlie book, *Charlie Plays Ball*, came out in March 2015.

DID YOU KNOW?
Actress Reese Witherspoon will play Drummond in the movie adaptation of Drummond's memoir.

BARNES & NOBLE

Events
bn.com/events

Ree Drummond
Monday, February 7th, 6PM

Drummond at a signing for *The Pioneer Woman* in 2011

Television Star

Drummond continued to earn fans with her books and **blog**. Eventually, producers at the Food Network took notice of her success. In November 2010, the network flew celebrity chef Bobby Flay to the Drummond ranch. He and Drummond had a **cook-off**. Drummond won the contest.

The Food Network gave Drummond her own show in 2011. It's called *The Pioneer Woman*. It is shot at the ranch. The Drummonds own a lodge a couple of miles from the family home. It is used for the show's set. The lodge has four bedrooms, so the crew can stay there while filming. This is especially helpful since the nearest hotel is quite a distance away!

In each **episode** of *The Pioneer Woman*, Drummond shows how to prepare some of her recipes. There is usually a theme, such as someone's birthday or a ranch activity. *The Pioneer Woman* allows viewers to escape to Drummond's picture-perfect ranch life for a while.

The kitchen in the lodge, where Drummond's TV show is filmed

Home on the Range

Drummond has always helped her husband run the ranch. In turn, Ladd helps Drummond with her business. He assists with her e-mails and takes care of the kids while she works. He also discusses possible **blog** posts with her. Drummond created a section of her website for Ladd. It's called "Marlboro Man," which is Drummond's nickname for him. Ladd writes posts for that section of the blog occasionally. But mostly, Drummond writes about him and his activities on the ranch.

Drummond spends a lot of time shooting her television show and appearing on other programs. She also goes on tours to promote her books. When she's home, Drummond cooks, cleans, and teaches the children while running her business.

Drummond is also an enthusiastic photographer, especially when it comes to food. She once published a cake recipe that had 53 photos! For fun, the Drummond family likes to play fantasy football. They also love to watch *The Amazing Race*.

Drummond spends time with her kids between taping episodes of her show.

Pioneer Perfection

Drummond has become a successful author, businesswoman, and reality TV star. Much of her success is due to how she presents her life. It is busy but also very organized and happy. She avoids comments about politics or cultural issues. Instead, Drummond talks about food, children, and simple, everyday things that everyone can understand. Even the design of her site reminds readers of a simpler, more wholesome time.

Drummond's work has influenced some people to try living more down-to-earth lives. The Pioneer Woman was named on a *Forbes* magazine list of 100 best websites for women.

Drummond never thought her life would turn as it has. "You can go ahead and feel free to make all the plans you want in life," she says. "But who knows where you'll really be in 15 or 20 years." Her fans hope she'll be at the ranch, sharing the recipes, photos, and family stories they've grown to love.

Although her life hasn't turned out as she planned, Drummond wouldn't change a thing!

Timeline

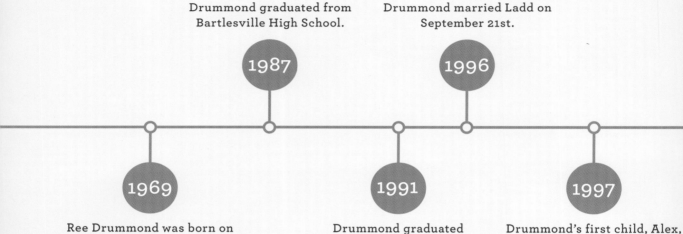

Drummond graduated from Bartlesville High School.

1987

Drummond married Ladd on September 21st.

1996

1969

Ree Drummond was born on January 6th in Bartlesville, Oklahoma.

1991

Drummond graduated from the University of Southern California.

1997

Drummond's first child, Alex, was born in June.

Ree Drummond Says

"I love most things country, because country, to me, is home."

"Make sure your passion shines through. It will show."

"I have a secret love. His name is The Country."

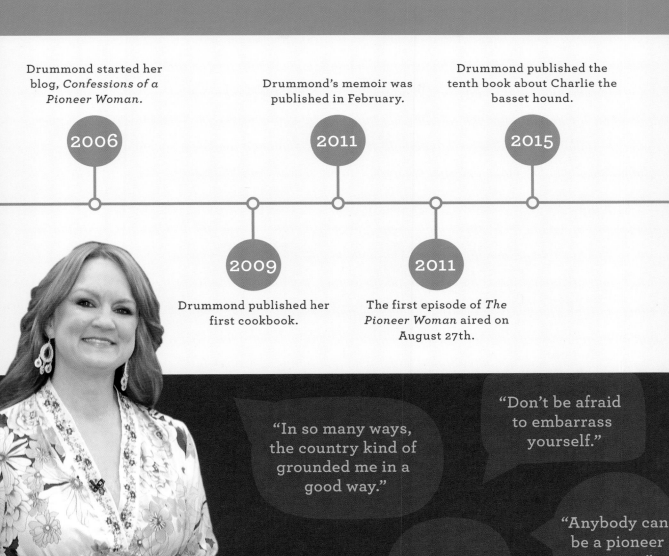

Drummond started her blog, *Confessions of a Pioneer Woman*.

2006

Drummond's memoir was published in February.

2011

Drummond published the tenth book about Charlie the basset hound.

2015

2009

Drummond published her first cookbook.

2011

The first episode of *The Pioneer Woman* aired on August 27th.

"In so many ways, the country kind of grounded me in a good way."

"Don't be afraid to embarrass yourself."

"Anybody can be a pioneer woman."

Glossary

basset hound – a breed of hunting dog that has short legs, very long ears, and a short, smooth coat.

blog – a website that tells about someone's personal opinions, activities, and experiences. A person who writes a blog is a blogger.

cook-off – a cooking contest.

episode – one show in a television series.

fold – to mix in an ingredient by gently and repeatedly lifting some of the mixture and laying it over the rest.

gerontology – the scientific study of old age and of the process of becoming old.

honeymoon – a trip or a vacation taken by a newly married couple.

isolation – the state of being separated from others.

journalism – the collecting and editing of news to be presented through various media. These include newspapers, magazines, television, and radio.

lifestyle – the way of a person, group, or society lives.

memoir – a written account of a person's experiences.

orthopedic surgeon – a doctor who specializes in operating on people to repair conditions affecting the bones or muscles.

sushi – a Japanese dish of cold cooked rice shaped in small cakes and topped or wrapped with other ingredients, such as pieces of raw fish.

vegetarian – one who lives on a diet consisting only of plant foods and sometimes fish, eggs, or dairy products.

Websites

To learn more about Reality TV Titans, visit **booklinks.abdopublishing.com**. These links are routinely monitored and updated to provide the most current information available.

Index